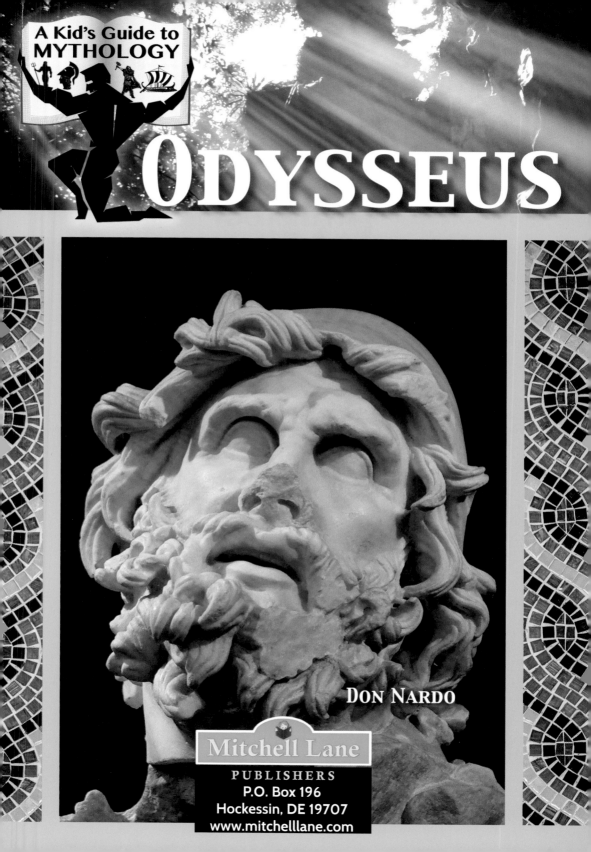

A Kid's Guide to
MYTHOLOGY

ODYSSEUS

Don Nardo

Mitchell Lane
PUBLISHERS
P.O. Box 196
Hockessin, DE 19707
www.mitchelllane.com

Mitchell Lane
PUBLISHERS

Printing   1   2   3   4   5   6   7   8

A Kid's Guide to
MYTHOLOGY

Apollo
Athena
Hercules
Jason

Odysseus
Poseidon
Thor
Zeus

Library of Congress Cataloging-in-Publication Data
Nardo, Don, 1947- author.
  Odysseus / by Don Nardo.
       pages cm. — (A kid's guide to mythology)
    Audience: Ages 8 to 11
  Audience: Grades 3 to 6
  Includes bibliographical references and index.
  ISBN 978-1-68020-006-5 (library bound)
1. Odysseus (Greek mythology)—Juvenile literature. 2. Mythology, Greek—Juvenile literature. 3. Troy (Extinct city)—Legends—Juvenile literature. I. Title.
BL820.O3N37 2015
292.1'3—dc23
                                                                      2015017161

eBook ISBN: 978-1-68020-007-2

CONTENTS

Words in **bold** throughout can be found in the Glossary.

The ancient Greek hero Odysseus as he appears on a pottery mixing bowl dating to the 300s BCE, *some 2,300 years ago.*

MYTHS AS MEMORIES

Odysseus (oh-DISS-ee-us) was one of the ancient Greeks' most famous and beloved heroes. The ancient Romans, who admired and eagerly copied Greek culture, were fond of him too. They called him Ulysses (yu-LISS-eez).

Also beloved by the Greeks and Romans was the great Greek poet and storyteller Homer (HO-mer). He wrote at length about Odysseus in two superb **epic poems**. The first, the *Iliad* (ILL-ee-ud), tells about the tenth year of the siege of Troy, a wealthy city in western **Anatolia** (what is now Turkey). The rulers of several Greek kingdoms made war on and eventually captured Troy. Among those kings was Odysseus, who ruled the Greek island realm of Ithaca (ITH-uh-kuh). Homer called him a very "capable man who journeyed across the world after seizing the proud fortress of Troy."[1]

That fateful, ten-year-long sea voyage is the subject of Homer's other masterpiece, the *Odyssey* (ODD-iss-ee). During the journey, Odysseus "endured numerous hardships," Homer said. He "fought to stay alive and to bring his shipmates home."[2]

The ancient Greek poet Homer, painted in 1509.

When the World Was Young

The Greeks who embraced the stories in Homer's epics lived in the several centuries following his lifetime. Homer's exact birth date is unknown. But most modern scholars think he lived in the 700s BCE, more than twenty-seven hundred years ago. The experts often call the residents of Greece in those centuries the "Classical Greeks." Their splendid achievements in art, architecture, and literature awed and inspired the generations that followed them. Greek civilization is now seen as the foundation of Western, or European-based, civilization, which includes the United States.

The Classical Greeks were captivated not only by Odysseus's exploits, but by many other myths as well. Part of the reason for this fascination was the setting of those tales. They took place in an ancient, extremely appealing, and almost magical era. The modern myth-teller Edith Hamilton described it as "a time when the world was young." In those days, she wrote, glorious heroes supposedly walked the earth. Believing this, the Classical Greeks called that era the "Age of Heroes." It was also said that mortal humans sometimes met the immortal gods face to face in that **mystical** realm. There was little difference "between the real and the unreal," Hamilton added. So the imagination was "vividly alive" in "that strangely and beautifully animated world."[3]

The Classical Greeks did not know how many centuries separated them from that special time and place in which Odysseus lived. Nor did they realize that many of their myths were dim, often garbled memories of a past Greek civilization. Modern historians call that earlier period of Greek culture the late **Bronze** Age. It lasted from about 1500 to 1100 BCE, ending roughly four centuries before Homer's time. It is called the Bronze Age because people then used tools and weapons made of bronze, a mixture of copper and tin. The Classical Greeks also had iron, at about 1050 BCE, which is a stronger, more durable metal.

During Greece's Bronze Age, a people now called the Minoans (my-NO-inz) dwelled on the big Greek island of Crete and some nearby islands. They had large fleets of ships. And with them they controlled the lands encircling the Aegean Sea, including mainland Greece.

Enormous Upheaval

On that mainland lived the Mycenaeans (my-sin-EE-unz). Modern historians named them after their fortress-town of Mycenae (my-SEE-nay), in southeastern Greece. It appears that for a while the Minoans dominated and culturally influenced the mainlanders. Then, in about 1450 BCE the Mycenaeans conquered Crete and the other Minoan-controlled islands.

The mainlanders prospered in the roughly two centuries that followed. In addition to taking over the region's trade routes, they raided towns on the coasts of Anatolia. One of those towns might have been Troy. In fact, Troy's ruins do indicate it underwent a siege in about 1180 BCE. That was shortly after the Mycenaeans were at their height of power. It remains uncertain whether the siege was the work of the Greeks. But if it was, the event might well have inspired the legend of the Trojan War.

It is certain that shortly after the assault in question, the Mycenaeans were themselves attacked. In about 1200 BCE, the entire Aegean region experienced enormous upheaval. So did many areas of the nearby Middle East. In the space of only a few short years, the cities of mainland Greece were wrecked and burned and the Mycenaean kingdoms crumbled. The exact reasons for this turmoil are still uncertain. But many experts think that large bands of warlike folk from the areas north of Greece swept southward—and they burned and looted every community in their path.

In whatever manner Minoan-Mycenaean civilization met its doom, its end left behind massive chaos and misery. The Greek world sank into a dark age of poverty and ignorance. Reading, writing, the arts, and the skills

These beautiful Minoan paintings from Akrotiri (on the island of Santorini, north of Crete) show Minoan oared ships carrying nobles.

of large-scale architecture were all lost. And over time, people forgot their **heritage**. This caused the memories of the events and important figures of their history to become increasingly distant and muddled. As the decades passed and became centuries, these fading memories changed into myths, and Greece's Bronze Age became the Age of Heroes.

One small light shining in the darkness of that age consisted of wandering poet-storytellers. Called *aoidoi* (a-ee-DEE), or bards, they kept those hazy memories of the past alive. Each bard memorized the stories. And some **tweaked** and/or added to them, too, so that the myths kept changing and evolving. The bards recited the stories to the residents of Greek villages, and most came to see them as real historical characters and events.

One of the Most Compelling Tales

Finally Homer, a true genius among those bards, came along. He brought two large collections of smaller myths—the *Iliad* and the *Odyssey*—to the height of popularity and beauty, and partly for that reason, the stories were soon written down. This was possible because the Greeks had emerged from the Dark Age around the time Homer was born. One of the achievements marking that event was the rediscovery of writing. Committing the epics to paper kept the myths from changing any further. So these first written versions are the ones that continue to be read, performed, and enjoyed today.

The Classical Greeks, who cherished those works, eventually departed history's stage. The Romans conquered and absorbed the Greek lands in the 200s and 100s BCE, and the two cultures merged into one **Greco-Roman** civilization, which ran its course and disappeared soon after Rome's fall in the 400s and 500s CE.

Yet many aspects of that brilliant society have survived, including most of its myths. Among them, Odysseus's story still stands out. Read for enjoyment, studied in schools, and repeatedly filmed, it remains one of the most compelling tales ever told. In the words of researcher Ernle Bradford, modern soldiers "have gone into battle with lines from Homer on their lips." And national leaders have quoted Odysseus "in grave debates and conferences." In addition, the stirring **saga** of Odysseus's wanderings has been "translated into almost every known language."[4]

DID NATURE AID THE INVADERS?

Modern historians have often debated why the Minoans were unable to fend off the invading Mycenaeans in the 1400s BCE. After all, the Minoans had large fleets of ships that controlled the seas. Why, then, were the Mycenaeans able to defeat the islanders so easily? Some scholars have suggested that the mainlanders were aided by a huge natural catastrophe. Its center was located on the island of Thera, today called Santorini. It lies about eighty miles (129 km) directly north of Crete, then the hub of Minoan society. Thera was mostly made up of a massive volcano, which violently erupted sometime between 1600 and 1450 BCE. Earthquakes leveled many Minoan buildings. Huge sea waves struck Crete and other Aegean islands, drowning thousands of people and destroying most of their ships and docks. Although the Minoans were able to survive the calamity, some scholars argue, it badly weakened them, and the aggressive Mycenaeans, who largely escaped the disaster, took advantage of that weakness.

Some of the Minoan ruins at Akrotiri, on Santorini.

A statue of Helen of Troy, from the ancient Greek city of Ephesus, on the western coast of what is now Turkey.

ODYSSEUS AT TROY

Odysseus's first great adventure was his involvement in the Trojan War. That epic fight had the same cause as many other human conflicts—men struggling over a beautiful woman. In this case, her name was Helen. She was wife to Menelaus (men-uh-LAY-us), ruler of the Greek kingdom of Sparta.

People far and wide agreed that Menelaus was a lucky man and the common wisdom was that Helen was the most stunning woman in the known world. Later, in the midst of the war, some Trojan men saw her, and according to Homer, they said, "This woman looks like an immortal goddess!"[1]

Evidence of His Madness

In fact, Helen was so beautiful that all of the Greek kings, including Odysseus, had once fallen in love with her. They also made a promise many of them would later regret. When Helen and Menelaus got engaged, the other kings swore they would all help him if another man stole her away.

As fate would have it, that was exactly what happened. One day Paris (PAIR-us), a prince of Troy, paid a visit to Sparta, and gazing upon Helen, he fell deeply in love with her. She had feelings for him, too, so he easily persuaded her to leave with him and run away to Troy.

When Menelaus found out what had happened, he was filled with rage. He hurried off to Mycenae, the Greek kingdom where his brother, Agamemnon (ag-uh-MEM-non), was king. Shocked at the news, Agamemnon agreed to lead a united Greek army to Troy and bring Helen back. He quickly sent messengers to the other Greek kings—among them Odysseus. Do not forget your oath, he told them, to give aid to Menelaus.

Several of the Greek rulers responded to this plea by assembling their soldiers and preparing to fight. But when Agamemnon's messenger arrived in Ithaca, it was a different story. Odysseus no longer pined for Helen. He had recently met and married a wonderful woman named Penelope (p'NELL-uh-pee), and fighting over another man's wife now seemed to him a waste of time, so he sent the messenger back with no reply. Unhappy about this snub, Agamemnon summoned Palamedes (pah-luh-MEE-deez), a Greek known for his wisdom. Go to Ithaca and convince Odysseus to change his mind, Agamemnon told Palamedes.

A while later, on Ithaca, Odysseus saw Palamedes approaching and correctly guessed why he had come. Thinking quickly, Odysseus pretended to be insane. Then he walked out into a field, with Palamedes at his heels. Odysseus yoked both an ox and a donkey to a plow and started working salt into the soil, something no farmer would ever do. This display was meant to be further evidence of his madness.

The Disguised Warrior

But wise Palamedes saw through the lie. He lifted Odysseus's infant son, Telemachus (tel-EM-uh-kiss), from a cradle and placed him right in the path of the ox and donkey. If Odysseus was sane, Palamedes reasoned, he would not allow his child to be crushed. Sure enough, at the last moment the royal plowman leapt forward and rescued Telemachus. Odysseus was forced to admit that he *was* perfectly sane. He agreed reluctantly to contribute twelve ships and six hundred soldiers to the assault on Troy.

It was now Odysseus's turn to persuade an unwilling warrior to fight. The man in question was Achilles (uh-KILL-eez), widely viewed as Greece's mightiest soldier. He was certainly not afraid to fight. But his mother had earlier heard a **prophecy**—a prediction made by a god that said that Achilles might someday die in a conflict with the Trojans. It therefore troubled her that the Greeks were preparing to attack Troy.

One of the many existing statues of Achilles.

She sent the young man to stay at his uncle's house, hoping no one would find him there. To make sure Achilles was well hidden, the uncle dressed him up in women's clothes.

No disguise could fool the cunning Odysseus, however. He discovered where Achilles was hiding and went there dressed as a poor merchant. The Ithacan king suspected that Achilles might be wearing female attire, so he brought along several women's products, including some perfume and eye makeup. Odysseus showed these to the household women, but when he did so, he made sure to slip a stout sword into the mix. Sure enough, one of the women ignored the feminine items and went right for the sword. In that way, the disguised merchant revealed the disguised warrior. After that, Odysseus swiftly convinced Achilles to join the upcoming expedition.

A Horrible Slaughter

The gathering of ships and soldiers soon crossed the wine-dark sea and the Greeks clashed with the Trojans in battle after battle. Weeks turned into months, and months into years, and still they fought. In one of the attacks, Odysseus roused his fellow Greeks to try harder. "We can fight the enemy more forcefully!" he shouted. "Be as tough as the sturdy bronze we wear to protect our bodies!"[2] Many on both sides died in that encounter and in others that followed. Yet even as the war entered its tenth year, there seemed no end in sight.

Finally, Odysseus managed to break the lethal deadlock. He told Agamemnon and the other kings that he had a plan to achieve total victory. In the days that followed, the Greeks secretly constructed a huge wooden horse. Then Odysseus and several other warriors hid inside its hollow belly. Leaving the towering object just outside the gates of Troy, the other Greeks boarded their ships and sailed away.

The Trojans assumed the war was over, and thinking that the horse was an offering to the gods they dragged it into the city and celebrated well into the night. Later, after they had finally fallen asleep, Odysseus and his companions climbed from the horse. They silently opened the gates and in rushed the rest of the Greeks, who had sailed back after sunset. A horrible slaughter ensued and proud Troy quickly fell.

An early modern painting shows the Trojan prince Hector (standing) urging his brother, Prince Paris, to join him in the next battle against the Greeks.

Odysseus now prepared for the trip back to Ithaca and an emotional reunion with his family. But the gods were not ready to allow that happy event to happen. They were angry over a terrible crime a Greek had committed during the fall of Troy. As a result, Odysseus and his men found themselves on the receiving end of divine **wrath**. For them, years of danger and terror lay ahead.

The Trojans drag the wooden horse into their city in this 1773 painting by Italian artist Giovanni Tiepolo.

ATHENA'S WRATH

A Greek warrior named Ajax (AY-jax) committed the terrible crime that angered the gods and kept Odysseus from going straight home. After Odysseus and his men opened Troy's gates, the Greeks went on a killing spree. They also looted the city. The gods fully expected such things to happen in wartime, but Ajax went too far. He barged into the local temple of Athena (uh-THEE-nuh), goddess of wisdom and war, where he found Cassandra (kuh-SAN-druh), daughter of Troy's king. She had knelt before Athena's sacred statue and asked for her protection. Ajax showed no respect for the goddess or her holy shrine. He cruelly raped the princess on the temple floor. Athena was rightly enraged by this awful act and decided to punish all the Greeks. At her request, Poseidon, the god of the seas, created an immense storm that struck the Greek ships during their homeward voyage. Ajax drowned. Nearly all of Agamemnon's vessels sank and Menelaus and his soldiers became lost, but later found themselves in faraway Egypt. Odysseus, it turned out, got the worst of it. He was forced to wander the seas for ten eventful, fearful years.

In the evening, after a hard day of fighting Trojans, two Greek warriors play a dice game.

A one-eyed giant prepares to destroy one of Odysseus's ships in this exciting scene from Homer's Odyssey.

3

CAVE OF THE CYCLOPS

The monstrous storm whipped up by the angry god Poseidon set in motion Odysseus's famous decade of wandering. The terrible tempest blew the twelve Ithacan ships far off course. "Those ill-fated winds pursued us for nine days," Odysseus said. "On the tenth day, however, we arrived in the land of the **Lotus** Eaters, people who live by eating that flower."[1]

The Lotus Eaters seemed harmless at first, but then they suggested that some of the Greeks try munching on the flowers. The men who did so quickly became forgetful. Even worse, they showed no more interest in returning to Greece. Odysseus and the others had to drag them back to the ships. "I ordered everyone to board and man the oars," Odysseus said. "And I warned that no one should eat the flowers. Or else they might no longer desire to go home."[2]

As If They Were Toys

Odysseus hoped they would not encounter any more weird and dangerous situations. But this turned out to be wishful thinking. They next landed on an island inhabited by a race of one-eyed giants—the Cyclopes (sy-KLOH-peez). Odysseus later described them as "a brutal, uncivilized race." They have no government or laws, he said, and "dwell in caves in the mountains." There, each Cyclops (SY-clops) "makes rules for himself and his family and has no concern for his neighbors."[3]

Odysseus hoped to avoid those **ogres**. So the plan was for him to lead only twelve men ashore and quietly gather some food and water. They would then hurry back to the ships and sail away unnoticed. About an hour into the mission, they came to a large cave. More than a dozen goats and sheep were penned up inside, and the men eagerly began collecting them.

Seemingly out of nowhere, however, the giant who dwelled in that cave appeared. His name, the Greeks later learned, was Polyphemus (pah-luh-FEE-mus). Before the men could escape, the Cyclops trapped them by blocking the entrance with a huge rock, and then he snatched up two of the Greeks as if they were toys. The giant smashed their heads against the floor, killing them. Next, he ripped their limp bodies apart and devoured them raw.

The other men were naturally horrified at this grisly spectacle. "We were powerless to stop it," Odysseus said. "All we could do was raise our hands to Zeus," leader of the gods, "and cry out for his aid!"[4] But no such help came. The Greeks spent a sleepless night as the Cyclops dozed and snored.

The next morning, Polyphemus butchered and ate two more of his captives. Then he departed, making sure the big rock was in place. Unable to move the boulder, Odysseus and the others remained trapped. That night, the giant came home, consumed two more Greeks, and washed them down with a bucket of wine. After that hideous meal, he turned to Odysseus. "Tell me your name!" Polyphemus insisted. The Ithacan king needed to employ all his famous cleverness now and he did so. "My name is Nobody," he answered. "My parents and everyone else call me Nobody."[5]

Pretending to be friendly, in order to fool the Cyclops, Odysseus pours the giant some wine.

Disaster Strikes

Odysseus displayed more of his cunning later, after the dreadful creature had fallen asleep. At their commander's orders, the six remaining crewmen sharpened a big wooden pole, and then they heated it in the fire. When the tip was glowing red, the men rammed it with all their might into Polyphemus's single eye. As smoke and blood shot out, the giant screamed in agony and leapt to his feet. He yanked the broiling beam from his tortured face, and then he loudly shouted in hopes of alerting the Cyclopes who lived in nearby caves.

A few minutes later, several of those monsters gathered outside, beyond the great stone that barred the entrance. "What's wrong, Polyphemus?" one of them asked. "Your loud cries are disturbing our sleep! Has someone tricked you or hurt you?" Remembering the name Odysseus had earlier given, Polyphemus blurted out. "Nobody!" he bellowed. "Nobody has tricked me! Nobody has injured me!"[6] When the other giants heard that "nobody" had hurt their neighbor, they turned and went home.

For the rest of the night, the Greeks carefully avoided the grasp of the cave's blinded owner. In the morning, following habit, Polyphemus rolled away the big rock so that his animals could go out and graze. When he did this, Odysseus and the others silently escaped. They hurried back to their ships and gladly left that frightening place far behind.

Unhappily for Odysseus, the six men who had been eaten marked only the beginning of his losses. After a while, the ships arrived at an island floating above the waves. This strange land belonged to the god of the winds, Aeolus (EE-oh-lus), who was a friendly deity. So

24

Aeolus ties off a bag containing powerful winds, which he is about to hand to Odysseus (in the red cape).

when Odysseus begged for his aid, he handed over a gift he claimed was useful. It was a hefty leather bag. In it, Aeolus said, were many of the fierce winds that often blew sailors off course. Keep those violent gales in the bag, the god ordered, and a gentle wind would push the ships back to Ithaca.

The Greeks at first followed the god's instructions. And sure enough, in only a week the hilltops of their beloved homeland appeared on the horizon. Thinking he could rest at last, Odysseus fell asleep. It was during his slumber that one of his men carelessly sliced open the bag. Immediately, an enormous storm exploded from it and drove the vessels backward into unknown seas.

There was nothing else to do, the disappointed Odysseus said, but to start searching for home from scratch. But only six days later, disaster struck. They came to an unknown island that was inhabited by huge cannibals. Hundreds of the bloodthirsty brutes swarmed the Greek ships, killing and eating everyone they could. Odysseus told the men on his **flagship**, "Grab your oars and row till your hearts crack!"[7]

Odysseus was thankful when they escaped. But all the other ships and men were lost. The saddened survivors sailed on, hoping to find a place free from danger where they might rest. They could not foresee that only more horror and death lay ahead.

THREE KINDS OF CYCLOPES

The one-eyed giants that Odysseus encountered during his wanderings were one of three kinds populating ancient Greek mythology. Those that Homer described in the *Odyssey* were said to be mean, vulgar, and uncultured. A second Greek tradition about Cyclopes claimed there existed some who were more civilized. Supposedly they dwelled on the Greek mainland in the very ancient past. Stout and diligent builders, they erected many massive stone walls. These included those of the imposing fortresses of the Bronze Age Mycenaeans. The early Classical Greeks were in awe of the remains of those structures. Surely, they thought, only giants could have built them. Seventh-century BCE Greek poet Hesiod (HESS-ee-id) recorded a third set of myths featuring Cyclopes. He wrote that the sky god Uranus and earth goddess Gaia had three one-eyed sons. Their names were Shiner (Arges/AR-gess), Thunderer (Brontes/BRON-tess), and Lightning-Maker (Steropes/STER-op-es). Uranus was afraid of those offspring, so he locked them away in a dark underground realm. Much later, Zeus, the leader of the Olympian gods, released them and they started making the thunderbolts that he hurled at his enemies.

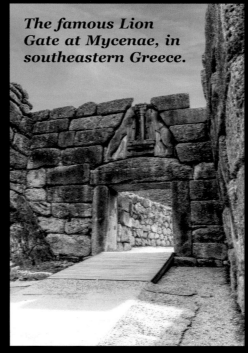

The famous Lion Gate at Mycenae, in southeastern Greece.

An early modern oil painting depicts Odysseus's first encounter with the witch Circe.

SLAYING THE SUITORS

During their wanderings, Odysseus and his men encountered a beautiful woman named Circe (SUR-see) on an island. She turned out to be a witch who turned people into pigs. This was the initial fate of some of Odysseus's crewmen. Luckily for them, the divine Hermes (HUR-meez) came to the Greeks' aid. Hermes was the messenger god and protector of travelers and he showed Odysseus how to resist Circe's magical spells. The defeated sorceress then agreed to change the pigs back into their human form.

After that, Circe and Odysseus came to trust each other. And when he was ready to leave her island, she offered some helpful advice. "There is only one way you can make it home," she said. Circe advised that Odysseus should "take an unusual detour—by way of the bitter houses of the dead."[1] Odysseus must contact a certain **shade**, or soul, in the Underworld, Circe told him—the spirit of Tiresias (ty-REE-see-us), who was once a wise old Greek. Tiresias would help Odysseus prepare for what he would find when he finally reached Ithaca.

CHAPTER 4

The Spirits of the Dead

Following Circe's instructions, the Greeks sailed to a deserted shore on the far edge of the world. They beached the ship and Odysseus hiked away into a nearby forest. After a while, he reached the place Circe had described. And there, he made **sacrifices**—offerings of milk, honey, and wine—to appease the gods and the dead.

This gesture of respect granted Odysseus a glimpse into a small sector of the dreary Underworld. He saw that the dimly lit region was crowded with human shades. Staggering around, zombie-like in the darkness were the spirits of people of all ages and walks of life. Some were folks he had known. There was King Agamemnon, for instance, who had led the Greeks at Troy. Odysseus also saw and spoke with his mother's soul. She had died of grief, she said, when he did not return from Troy.

Eventually, old Tiresias's shade appeared. He told Odysseus that the remainder of the homeward voyage would not be easy. But he *would* make it to Ithaca. There, however, he would find trouble. A group of local noblemen were demanding that his loving wife, Penelope, marry one of them. They were "ill-mannered men," Tiresias said.[2] "They eat up your cattle and sheep while wooing your queen." In addition, these **suitors** wanted more than just Penelope. Each also longed to possess Odysseus's throne and royal treasury.

This disturbing news made Odysseus more determined than ever to reach home. He swiftly returned to the ship and he and his men set sail. After a while, they recognized that they were in the Mediterranean Sea. They knew its waters would in time merge with the waters that surrounded their island home—and they began to have hope.

Sealing Their Own Fates

But it was only Odysseus who was destined to set foot again on Ithaca. Giant monsters and angry gods robbed him of his last ship and the rest of his crew. Yet after ten long years, countless hardships, and exhaustion, Odysseus did make it home. There, he quickly found that the shade of old Tiresias had been right. Most Ithacans thought their once-popular king had died long ago, and his faithful wife endured the continued unwanted advances of dozens of suitors.

Odysseus later learned that Penelope had managed to fend off those rascals for several years. Before choosing one of them, she said, she had to finish weaving a **tapestry** in her bedchamber. Each day she wove some of that tapestry, but each evening she unraveled the sections she had earlier completed; the tapestry was never finished. The problem was that recently the suitors had learned about her trick, and now their demands that she pick one of them had become insistent and mean-spirited.

Odysseus planned to rid his palace of those villains, but first he needed to make allies to prepare for his fight against the suitors. Disguising himself as a poor beggar, he tracked down his now grown son, Telemachus. After their tearful reunion, the young man led his father into the palace's banquet hall. There, the suitors were partying and drinking the royal wine cellars dry. Seeing Odysseus, they assumed he was a mere beggar. Typical cowards and bullies, they laughed at him and pelted him with

In an engraving from the early 1800s, the excited Odysseus (standing at far left) catches sight of his son Telemachus (in the doorway with his hounds).

food scraps. They had no idea that they had sealed their own fates.

The next morning the suitors gathered as usual in the banquet hall. Quietly, Odysseus, Telemachus, and the servants who had remained loyal bolted the doors from the outside. Odysseus walked to the center of the room, threw off his beggar's garb, and brandished his mighty bow. He called the suitors "yellow dogs" who had "abused my servants and pursued my wife while I still lived." For those crimes, he said, "your blood will now spill."[3]

Suddenly panic-stricken, the suitors ran back and forth like scared chickens. Try as they might, they could not shield themselves from Odysseus's fast-flying arrows. Telemachus and the servants, who were armed with swords, hacked down the rest of the terrified men. Within a few minutes, every suitor lay still. In Homer's words, their eyes clouded over with "the fog of death."[4]

Only after slaying the suitors and restoring order and honor in his house did Odysseus reveal himself to his

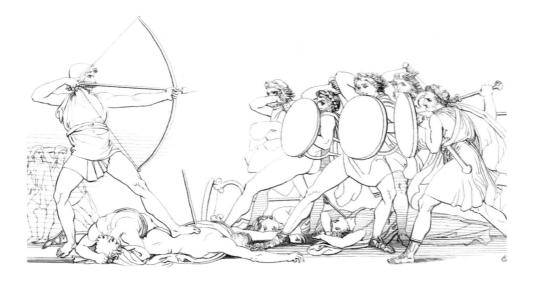

Armed with his mighty bow, Odysseus slays the suitors one by one.

Still dressed as a lowly beggar, Odysseus chats with Penelope, who had never lost hope that they would one day be reunited.

beloved Penelope. The two lovers were together again after twenty years apart. In all that time, neither had given up hope that they would someday be reunited. They were overcome with joy in what they deemed a perfect moment in time. The dazzling Athena sensed this and, using her divine powers, she prolonged that happy moment by holding back the coming dawn.

HIS MASTER'S VOICE

Homer's *Odyssey* contains one of the most touching scenes in Western literature. Not long before leaving for the Trojan War, Odysseus had taken a new puppy into his house. He had named him Argus. As dog and master so often do, they became instant friends and they seemed inseparable. But Odysseus's departure for Troy did separate them. During the long years that followed, Argus never forgot the man he saw as his father. Ever loyal, he waited and waited for him to return. Argus grew old and the palace servants who used to groom him eventually abandoned him. When Odysseus finally returned to Ithaca, he approached the palace. As Homer told it, he saw an aged hound lying in a pile of donkey manure. "There lay Argus, covered with flies. Suddenly he heard his master's voice." His father had at last come home. Joyfully, "he wagged his tail and dropped his ears. But he no longer had the strength to get up," so he used his eyes and, "after twenty years of waiting, he looked upon his beloved master." Then faithful Argus slowly shut his eyes "as death's dark hand closed over him."[5]

An engraving from the 1600s shows the aged dog Argus recognizing his master, Odysseus, after the

Noted actor Kirk Douglas played Odysseus in the 1954 film Ulysses.

5

ODYSSEUS IN POPULAR CULTURE

Odysseus's story was already a literary classic in the era of the Classical Greeks and it remains so today. The passage of more than twenty-five centuries has not dulled its sparkle as an exciting story of adventure, nor has time lessened its impact on Western thought and culture. Today Odysseus and his wanderings are deeply embedded in popular culture, which includes novels, games, toys, music, plays, television shows, and films.

Too Important to Die
The original mythical stories of Odysseus were told in the *Iliad* and the *Odyssey*. Those epics by Homer are now viewed as the first major examples of Western literature. But they were more than just well written books to the Classical Greeks. They viewed Homer's works much like medieval Christians saw the Bible—as a blueprint for life and society.

The *Iliad* and the *Odyssey* inspired Greek artists. Thousands of statues and wall and vase paintings showed Odysseus and other Homeric gods and heroes. Greek philosophers and elders pointed to numerous moral ideals and lessons from the epics, and Greek children memorized and recited Homer's verses at school. They knew Odysseus, Athena, the Cyclops, and Achilles like young people today know Captain Kirk, Harry Potter, Darth Vader, and Spiderman. Overall, one modern expert says, the Greeks believed Homer's works "contained whatever knowledge" most people "could need." The *Odyssey* alone described "war and peace, the crafts and skills, diplomacy and politics, wisdom, courtesy, courage," and duties toward "parents and the gods."[1]

As a result, Homer's epics, in which Odysseus's tale looms large, proved too important to die. The stories easily survived the fall of Rome and the end of ancient times. In the medieval era that followed, Christianity replaced the traditional Greco-Roman faiths in Europe so people no longer worshiped Zeus, Athena, and the other gods who appear in Homer's epics. Yet Europeans held onto most of the ancient myths. This was partly because Christian teachers used Odysseus's story and other old myths to help teach moral lessons. Thus, these tales remained part of the cultural background of Western civilization.

In addition, Homer's characters, including Odysseus, became the subjects of great artists. From wall paintings that date to the first century CE and oil paintings that date from the 1300s on up to the present, hundreds of drawings and paintings based on Odysseus's exploits have graced museums and private homes. One is *The Return of Odysseus*, by the Italian master Pinturicchio. Painted in 1509, it shows the long-absent Ithacan king greeting his wife Penelope.

Another Italian, Pellegrino Tibaldi, was also fascinated by Homer's *Odyssey*. His 1550 canvas, *The Blinding of Polyphemus*, is one of many paintings showing Odysseus's encounter with the Cyclops. *In the Cave of Polyphemus*

(1635), by Belgian artist Jacob Jordaens, is another. Many recent painters have also illustrated Odysseus's myth. A fine example is African-American artist Romare Bearden's 1978 version of Odysseus's return—*The Return of Ulysses*.

The Best Story Ever Written

Among the many musical adaptations of Odysseus's tale, one of the earliest was the three-act opera *Odysseus* composed by Claudio Monteverdi in 1640; it is still performed. Much later, in 1873, German composer

Jordaens's 1635 painting, titled In the Cave of Polyphemus, *shows Odysseus trying to reason with the Cyclops.*

Max Bruch composed a work titled *Odysseus*, which is scored for orchestra and choir. English composer Malcolm Arnold used the same approach in his 1976 work, *The Return of Odysseus*.

It is an even bigger leap from the pages of Homer to the Broadway stage. But that leap was made in 1954 when the musical play *The Golden Apple* opened in New York City. Including scenes from both the *Iliad* and the *Odyssey*, it received positive reviews. Less fortunate was *Home Sweet Homer*, a 1975 Broadway musical of the *Odyssey*. On the plus side, it starred the famous stage and film actor Yul Brynner as Odysseus. On the negative side, the critics panned it and it closed after its first performance.

Critical reception was very different for the most famous novel based on the *Odyssey*. Irish writer James Joyce

published *Ulysses* in 1922. (Joyce chose to use the Roman version of Odysseus's name.) The plot of this widely loved modern classic revolves around a man named Leopold Bloom. His travels through the streets of

The great Irish novelist James Joyce in 1915.

Dublin, Ireland, parallel those of Odysseus in Homer's original story.

Especially popular are the filmed versions of Odysseus's exploits. The earliest was a French silent film made in 1905—*Ulysses and the Giant Polyphemus*. The first major sound film based on the *Odyssey* was made in Italy in 1955. Called *Ulysses*, it featured the noted American actor Kirk Douglas in the title role. Its budget was fairly low, but the filmmakers were ambitious and included many major scenes from Homer's epic. The most effective scenes in the film are the deadly meeting with the Cyclops and the battle with the suitors.

A year after that movie's release, Odysseus's character appeared in another film based on Homer. This one was a big-budget Hollywood production—*Helen of Troy*. British-born actor Torin Thatcher, who emphasized the character's cleverness, played Odysseus. A later film version of Odysseus's story was a 1997 TV miniseries titled *The Odyssey*. Starring Armand Assante as the strong and brave Ithacan king, it features excellent, believable special effects.

Many other variations on Odysseus's tale exist in American, British, and other areas of Western popular culture. And there is little doubt that new ones will be created in the future. It is only natural to ask why the story remains so popular. The late W.H.D. Rouse, whose translation of the *Odyssey* is widely respected, suggested a reason. "This is the best story ever written," he said. No other has such a mix of adventure, heroics, battles, monsters, magic, lust, love, and human interaction with the divine. As a result, Rouse wrote, "It enchants" every person "who hears it."[2]

CREATING STUNNING ILLUSIONS

One of the most compelling moments in Odysseus's story is his run-in with the Cyclops. That scene has always been a special challenge for filmmakers. Homer described Polyphemus as a giant. And it is essential to make the audience believe that the onscreen Cyclops does indeed tower over Odysseus and the other Greeks. That illusion has been achieved in various ways. One is called a "**forced perspective** shot." The director and camera operator first place the actor playing the Cyclops in one spot. Then they put the Greeks in the shot, but have them stand farther away from the camera than Polyphemus. Photographing everyone together can create a stunning illusion. If the actors are carefully positioned, they all appear to be the same distance from the camera, yet the Greeks look smaller than the Cyclops. Another method is called **CGI** (Computer Generated Imagery). First, the actor playing Polyphemus is filmed standing in the cave. This image is scanned into a computer. A separate shot of the Greeks standing in the cave is also scanned in. Then a technician combines the two images, making sure to make the Cyclops tower over the men.

Odysseus (in the foreground) and his men warily observe the Cyclops in the cave scene from the 1954 film Ulysses.

CHAPTER NOTES

All translations of the *Iliad* and the *Odyssey* in this volume are by the author, Don Nardo.

Chapter 1: Myths as Memories
1. Homer, *Odyssey* 1.2–5.
2. Ibid, 1.8–10.
3. Edith Hamilton, *Mythology* (New York: Grand Central, 1999), 13.
4. Ernle Bradford, *Ulysses Found* (Charleston, SC: History Press, 2005), viii.

Chapter 2: Odysseus at Troy
1. Homer, *Iliad* 3.187–191.
2. Ibid, 19.274–275.

Chapter 3: Cave of the Cyclops
1. Homer, *Odyssey* 9.83–86.
2. Ibid, 9.100–102.
3. Ibid, 9.107, 115–117.
4. Ibid, 9.294–295.
5. Ibid, 9. 354–356, 366–367.
6. Ibid, 9.399–403, 406.
7. Ibid, 10.126.

Chapter 4: Slaying the Suitors
1. Homer, *Odyssey* 10.491, 493–495.
2. Ibid, 11.121–122.
3. Ibid, 22.36–39, 42.
4. Ibid, 22.89.
5. Ibid, 17.300–305, 333–335.

Chapter 5: Odysseus in Popular Culture
1. Robert Flaceliere, *Daily Life in Greece at the Time of Pericles* (London: Phoenix, 1996), 97.
2. Quoted in Homer, *Odyssey*, trans. W.H.D. Rouse (New York: Signet, 1999), vii.

WORKS CONSULTED

Bellingham, David. *An Introduction to Greek Mythology*. Secaucus, NJ: Chartwell Books, 1989.

Bowra, C.M. *Classical Greece*. New York: Time-Life, 1977.

Bradford, Ernle. *Ulysses Found*. Charleston, SC: History Press, 2005.

Burkert, Walter. *Greek Religion, Archaic and Classical*. Oxford, England: Basil Blackwell, 1985.

Drews, Robert. *The End of the Bronze Age: Changes in Warfare and the Catastrophe ca. 1200 B.C.* Princeton: Princeton University Press, 1995.

Finley, M.I. *The World of Odysseus*. New York: New York Review, 2002.

Fitten, J. Lesley. *Discovery of the Greek Bronze Age*. London: British Museum Press, 1995.

Grant, Michael. *A Guide to the Ancient World*. New York: Barnes and Noble, 1997.

Grant, Michael. *The Myths of the Greeks and Romans*. New York: Plume, 1995.

Grant, Michael and John Hazel. *Who's Who in Classical Mythology*. London: Routledge, 2002.

Griffin, Jasper. *Homer: The Odyssey*. New York: Cambridge University Press, 1987.

Hamilton, Edith. *Mythology*. New York: Grand Central, 1999.

Howatson, M.C. and Ian Chilvers, eds. *The Concise Oxford Companion to Classical Literature*. New York: Oxford University Press, 2007.

Latacz, Joachim. *Troy and Homer: Towards a Solution of an Old Mystery*. New York: Oxford University Press, 2004.

Levi, Peter. *The Penguin History of Greek Literature*. New York: Penguin, 1987.

Martin, Thomas R. *Ancient Greece: From Prehistoric to Hellenistic Times*. New Haven: Yale University Press, 2000.

Matyszak, Philip. *The Greek and Roman Myths: A Guide to the Classical Stories*. London: Thames and Hudson, 2010.

Morford, Mark P.O. and Robert J. Lenardon, *Classical Mythology*. New York: Oxford University Press, 2010.

Rouse, W.H.D. *Gods, Heroes and Men of Ancient Greece*. New York: New American Library, 2001.

Solomon, Jon. *The Ancient World in the Cinema*. New Haven: Yale University Press, 2001.

Stapleton, Michael. *The Illustrated Dictionary of Greek and Roman Mythology*. New York: Peter Bedrick, 1986.

Webster, T.B.L. *From Mycenae to Homer*. New York: Routledge, 2014.

Wood, Michael. *In Search of the Trojan War*. London: BBC, 2005.

FURTHER READING

Connolly, Peter. *The Legend of Odysseus*. New York: Oxford University Press, 2005.

Daly, Kathleen N. *Greek and Roman Mythology A to Z*. New York: Chelsea House, 2009.

Green, Roger L. *Tales of the Greek Heroes*. London: Puffin, 2009.

The following translations of Homer's *Iliad* and *Odyssey* are widely viewed as among the finest available:

Homer, *Iliad*. Translated by Robert Fagles. New York: Penguin, 2009.

Homer, *Iliad*. Translated by E.V. Rieu. New York: Penguin, 2003.

Homer, *Iliad*. Translated by W.H.D. Rouse. New York: Signet, 2007.

Homer, *Odyssey*. Translated by Robert Fagles. New York: Penguin, 2006.

Homer, *Odyssey*. Translated. Richmond Lattimore. New York: Harper, 2007.

Homer, *Odyssey*. Translated by E.V. Rieu. New York: Penguin, 2003.

Homer, *Odyssey*. Translated by W.H.D. Rouse. New York: Signet, 2007.

Warner, Rex. *Men and Gods*. New York: NYRB, 2008.

ON THE INTERNET

Ancient Greece, "Greek Life as Depicted in Homer's Epic: The Odyssey."
http://www.ancientgreece.com/essay/v/greek-life-as-depicted-in-homers-epic-the-odyssey/

Encyclopedia Mythica, "Odysseus."
http://www.pantheon.org/articles/o/odysseus.html

Greek Mythology.com, "The Odyssey, translated by Samuel Butler."
http://www.greekmythology.com/Books/Odyssey/odyssey.html

Greek Mythology Link, "Helen."
http://www.maicar.com/GML/Helen.html

Greek Mythology Link, "Odysseus."
http://www.maicar.com/GML/Odysseus.html

Greek Mythology Link, "Paris."
http://www.maicar.com/GML/Paris.html

Mythweb, "The Odyssey, a Short Version."
http://www.mythweb.com/odyssey/background_s.html

Theoi Greek Mythology,"Circe (Kirke)."
http://www.theoi.com/Titan/Kirke.html

Theoi Greek Mythology, "Polyphemos."
http://www.theoi.com/Gigante/GigantePolyphemos.html

Theoi Greek Mythology, "Zeus."
http://www.theoi.com/Olympios/Zeus.html

PHOTO CREDITS: All design elements from Thinkstock/Sharon Beck. Cover, p. 1—Jastrow/Public Domain; pp. 4, 6, 7, 9, 17, 18, 23, 25, 28, 33, 34, 35, 39, 40—cc-by-sa; p. 11—Dreamstime © Devilfire; p. 15—Dreamstime © Maocheng; p. 19—Thinkstock; p. 20—Dreamstime © Philcold; p. 27—Dreamstime © Elgreko74; p. 32—Newscom/akg-images; p. 36—Newscom/picture-alliance; p. 42—Newscom/SNAP/REX.

GLOSSARY

Anatolia (an-uh-TOLL-ya)—also called Asia Minor; the large land mass today comprising the nation of Turkey. In ancient times, its western sector, bordering the Aegean Sea, was a Greek cultural area

aoidoi (a-ee-DEE)—in ancient Greece, roving minstrels, bards, or storytellers

bronze (bronz)—a mixture of copper and tin

CGI (see-gee-EYE)—Computer Generated Imagery—a movie special effects method in which two groups of people or objects are filmed separately and those pieces of film are scanned into a computer. There, the pieces are combined in such a way that both groups of people or objects look like they were photographed in the same place at the same time

epic poem (epik POH-um)—a long literary work, told in verse and having larger-than-life characters and serious themes such as war, heroism, or human destiny

flagship (FLAG-ship)—the primary or commanding vessel in a fleet

forced perspective (fors'd per-SPEK-tiv)—a movie special effects method in which people or objects in the foreground are photographed alongside people or objects in the background in such a way that they look like they are standing beside one another

Greco-Roman (grek-oh-ROH-min)—having to do with the merger of the ancient Greek and Roman civilizations during and after Rome's conquest of the Greek kingdoms and city-states in the 200s and 100s BCE

heritage (HAIR-uh-tij)—the origins or background of a person, place, or thing

lotus (LOH-tis)—a water plant with an attractive flower, native to southern Asia. The lotus flower Homer described in the *Odyssey* was probably the ziziphus lotus, which grows in the Mediterranean region

mystical (MIS-ti-kl)—mysterious and/or magical

ogre (OH-ger)—a gruff, mean old man; or as often portrayed in fictional literature, a bad-tempered and/or dangerous giant, a monster

prophecy (PRAH-fuh-see)—a prediction about future events

sacrifice (SAK-ruh-fice)—an offering made to appease a god or gods

saga (SAH-guh)—a long, larger-than-life story or drama

shade—in ancient Greco-Roman culture, the soul or spirit of a dead person

suitor (SUE-ter)—a man who seeks to marry a woman

tapestry (TAP-iss-tree)—a decorated cloth drape or wall hanging, often woven

tweak (TWEEK)—to make small changes in something

wrath (rath)—anger

INDEX

ABOUT THE
AUTHOR

Historian and award-winning writer Don
Nardo has published more than four
hundred books for teens and children,
along with a number of volumes for
college and general adult readers. His
specialty is the ancient world, including
the histories, cultures, and myths of
the Greeks, Romans, and peoples of
Mesopotamia. Nardo also composes and
arranges orchestral music. He lives with
his wife Christine in Massachusetts.